ON
THE
WALL

ON THE WALL

A devotional for Medical Professionals

DR. LESLIE-ANN WILLIAMS M.D.

All scripture quotations unless otherwise indicated are from the NKJV Copyright ©1982 Thomas Nelson, Inc.

Scripture quotations are taken from the Holy Bible, New Living Translation, copyright ©1996, 2004, 2007, 2013, 2015 by Tyndale House Foundation. Used by permission of Tyndale House Publishers, Inc., Carol Stream, Illinois 60188. All rights reserved.

Scripture quotations taken from the Amplified® Bible (AMP), Copyright © 2015 by The Lockman Foundation
Used by permission. www.lockman.org.
Scripture taken from the NEW AMERICAN STANDARD BIBLE®, Copyright © 1960, 1962, 1963, 1968, 1971, 1972, 1973, 1975, 1977, 1995 by The Lockman Foundation. Used by permission

This book includes information from many sources and personal experiences. It is intended to be used as a guide and a resource for its readers and is not intended to replace or substitute professional counseling or therapy where necessary. The publisher and author do not claim any responsibility or liability, directly or indirectly, for information or advice presented. While accuracy and completeness of the material, we claim no responsibility for potential inaccuracies, omissions, incompleteness, error, or inconsistencies.

Printed and bound in the United States of America.
Bulk Ordering Information: Special discounts are available on quantity purchases by U.S. Trade Bookstores, wholesalers, corporations, non-profit organizations, associations, and others. For further details, contact publisher Leslie-Ann Williams, M.D below.

By email: lesliewilliamsmd@gmail.com
Social Media Forums:
(Facebook, Instagram, and Twitter) @DrLeslieAnnMD

During these times of COVID, the need for prayer became even more important to sustain. We have worked tirelessly, and we have been tired, some are discouraged, some are afraid, many have lost loved ones and colleagues. It has been an all-out assault on our sensitivities and our souls. The strength that we need is beyond ourselves and this is why we turn to the Lord.

We can allow unprecedented circumstances to build us or to break us. I am convinced that if you are reading this, you are part of the BUILD team.

In 2015, I started a prayer community called On the Wall. It is made up of all black female physicians from around the world. As black female physicians, the support we need is not always afforded us and so this community has been a lifeline for many. The guiding scripture is taken from the book of Nehemiah as he was rebuilding the wall. In Nehemiah 4:14, it says

> *Then as I looked over the situation, I called together the nobles and the rest of the people and said to them, "Don't be afraid of the enemy! Remember the Lord, who is great and glorious, and fight for your brothers, your sons, your daughters, your wives, and your homes!"*

And so, I encourage us, as we look over this situation in our world today, to not be afraid. Be community minded and fight for each other. If we all stand up and have the back of our neighbor, no-one is left uncovered. As I wrote this book, I was encouraged. It also encouraged me to encourage others. Be strong and very courageous for Our God is with us.

CONTENTS

1

I Surrender

Galatians 2:20 I have been crucified with Christ and I no longer live, but Christ lives in me; and the life which I now live in the flesh I live by faith in the Son of God, who loved me and gave Himself up for me.

Surrender typically conjures up images of defeat. When an army surrenders, they usually surrender to their enemy and it is a deafest. They could not withstand the power of the opponent. As a believer however, our surrender is a victory. We are surrendering to a power greater than us, that is the Lord; and not just any Lord, but our Lord, Jesus Christ. In our case we are surrendering to someone who LOVES us and demonstrated it by giving His very life that WE may live! So, our surrender is not a demise, it is a demonstration of our trust that He will do better with our life than we can do for ourselves. It is amazing to think of this, but God loves us with such an amazing love.

We all have or have heard of stories of patients who needed an amputation or a mastectomy but refused because they were afraid and held on to the diseased parts due likely to fear, to their demise.

Let me share this story with you. She walked into my office having heard that I prayed for patients and believed that God would heal her. She walked in holding her chest as she looked down. Our eyes barely met. As we spoke, I learned that she was diagnosed with breast cancer albeit she was reluctant to tell me her diagnosis, as though speaking it would make it real. I spoke it, "So you were diagnosed with breast cancer?" She believed that God would heal her and so she refused any treatment as she desired "divine healing". As she spoke, I prayed silently asking the Lord what to say to her. I knew what the science said but I also knew that my God was able to do the impossible. The question was what would be the case for her? She held on to a diseased breast and in essence sacrificed her whole life. She had in essence boxed God into working in ONLY one way. Sadly, she did not survive. I believe in divine healing as well and I also know that there are times that we have to surrender some things in order to get that which we desire. We have to release what is in our hand and relinquish control to allow Him to have total control. We hold on to things so tight thinking that what we have is so great, but His gift for us is so much better. I pray that today, you will surrender it all to Him.

Prayer: Lord today as I go about my day, I give everything that I am. You are my Creator and you know me better than I know myself. I pray Father that today I remember that you love me more than I could ever love myself. I surrender my successes, my failures, my looks my likes, my talents…my everything into your loving arms. Take control as I meet with my patients. Help me to share your power with them. In Jesus Name. Amen.

Prayer Journal: What will you surrender to the Lord today?

2

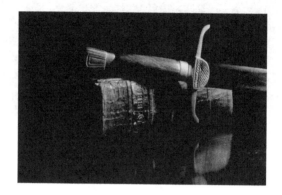

Praise is a weapon

Psalm 149:5-9 Let the godly ones exult in glory; let them sing for joy on their beds. Let the high praises of God be in their throats, and a two-edged sword in their hands, to execute vengeance on the nations and punishment on the peoples, to bind their kings with chains, and their nobles with fetters of iron, to execute on them the judgment written. This is the honor for all His godly ones. Praise the Lord! (Hallelujah!)

In the early 90s, I was in a church meeting, one we call a revival and a woman was leading the praise and worship. She said something that has stuck with me almost 30 years later. PRAISE IS A WEAPON. It shifted my mindset about praise. Now, I am acutely aware every time I clap my hands, raise my voice, stomp my feet that I am wreaking havoc on the enemy's camp! My praise is effectual. It also changes my perspective because once I elevate Christ, I am no longer fighting from my vantage point because my vantage point is limited. From my vantage point, I only see one tile, but Christ on the other hand, sees the entire floor plan! Once I elevate Christ, I am fighting from a position of victory. I am seated in heavenly places with Christ Jesus. Christ is fighting with AND for me, front back, side, side, top, and bottom. He has got me and you! It is no coincidence that whenever the Israelites went out to fight, the Levites lead the way with praise and worship.

Every battle was covered in praise and worship. It should be no different in this time. When we lead with praise, we position ourselves to fight from a position of VICTORY.

Consider our medical team our army today. As in the army there are specialists, so in medicine each specialist is laser focused; striking at the enemy and having success requires laser focused precision. Each person has their distinct role, and together we fight the enemy which is disease. As physicians, we fight for our patients fervently and we have to realize that our fierce conviction truly impacts our patients. We fight the disease from all ends, from a spiritual as well as a physical end. So today as we enter into our respective assignments, let us know that we are not just using natural weapons, let us use spiritual weapons and speak life over our patients.

Prayer: Lord thank you that the weapons of my warfare are not carnal but mighty through God for the pulling down of strongholds. Thank you, Lord, that as I position myself today, I lift You up. I thank you that you go before me always and as I stay in your Presence I am protected. Thank you for my team and thank you for the team of angels you have set around me. Thank you, Lord, for the victory. In Jesus Name, Amen.

Prayer Journal: What changes in you when you truly praise and worship the Lord?

3

Even Now

John 11:20 When Martha heard that Jesus was coming, she went to meet Him while Mary remained sitting in the house. Martha then said to Jesus, Master, if You had been here, my brother would not have died. And even now I know that whatever You ask from God He will grant it to you.

Have you ever had an attitude with the Lord because He did not do something in your timeframe? I know I am not the only one guilty of this. He did not do it HOW we wanted it done with WHOM we wanted it done, WHEN we wanted it done. He was just lapsing! Like God?! What's up with that?! BUT remember He is God. The awesome thing about the Lord is that He understands our human foibles and he does not change because of our emotions or inconsistencies. He is not insecure about His abilities nor shaken when we challenge Him.

I have found that God sometimes waits until the LAST minute, in our timeframe to do things! It's as though He wants to see if our faith will stay firm.

There are times when I start a medication on Monday, and the patient expects to see drastic change by Monday night! I have to remind them that healing does not always happen instantaneously. It is not always on their time, but it is IN time. As physician professionals, we do not always have the answers. We sometimes question ourselves about the right therapies but let us purpose today to walk confidently into the room and take Him with us because He sees and knows all things. Whenever Jesus walks into a room, everything changes. We are His hands and feet; we bring Him in the room. Let us be confident that even now, after we have studied and showed ourselves approved, we can rely on His adding to the work we have done and making it great.

> **Prayer:** Dear Lord, thank you that you are the God of time and you exist outside of time. Thank you also Father that you are always right on time. In fact, you have already crafted and placed everything in time. I pray Lord that you will give me eyes to see you clearly and ears to hear you clearly. I trust you to show up and show out. In Jesus Name, Amen.

Journal: When in your life have you felt God was taking too long or had forgotten you? How did it turn out?

4

Invite Him in Your Boat

John 6:16-21: When evening came, his disciples went down to the lake, where they got into a boat and set off across the lake for Capernaum. By now it was dark, and Jesus had not yet joined them. A strong wind was blowing, and the waters grew rough. When they had rowed about three or four miles, they saw Jesus approaching the boat, walking on the water; and they were frightened. But he said to them, "It is I; don't be afraid." Then they were willing to take him into the boat, and immediately the boat reached the shore where they were heading.

Times of transition can be so scary. The place in between what was and what will be is terrifying for even the brave among us. The disciples were in the boat and the wind was strong and the waters rough, all of this in the dark can absolutely cause one to lose faith.

In medicine, we experience and undergo many transitions, we go from medical student to resident to attending physician/consultant. With each of these transitions, we encounter uncertainty. I remember as a medical student, I was so nervous about knowing the information, passing exams, actually BECOMING a doctor. Then I started clinical rounds and just being IN the hospital was intimidating but the more I went the less intimidating it was. The more I trusted, the less I feared. As a resident I thought, "goodness I have to teach medical students!", I did not believe I knew much, but I continued to walk in faith. And even when residency became hard and challenging on a physical and emotional level, I continued to turn to the source of my strength, my relationship with the Lord. And so, it continued, with every transition, my confidence was challenged but with each transition, I invited Jesus into my boat. At every juncture, I have had to remind myself that God called me to this, and I would be strong and courageous. And if he called me to it, He has equipped me for it.

As a black woman in medicine, I have had lies told about me that was crafted to jeopardize my completing my medical training. I have been in the midst of the storm where the only hope was to hold on to Christ and draw strength from Him. I have cried many tears during my times of transition. I believe that those tears landed on the ground and formed roots, because after every storm I was able to stand taller, with more confidence, with more conviction, with a deeper resolve. And so, can you.

As we master our own transitions, we are given the opportunity to help our patients navigate their own health transitions. Redirecting their fears and stirring up faith in them. We can apply the faith that we used in our trials to strengthen and encourage our patients and colleagues.

PRAYER: Father thank you for the seasons you have orchestrated in my life. Thank you that you are my rock and my salvation, and you are with me in the good and bad times. Father even when things are not always good, you remain GOD. As I navigate these strong winds, cause me to launch my sails of peace. I invite you into my boat Lord. In Jesus Name, Amen.

Prayer Journal: What boat are you in now? Have you invited Jesus in? How can you invite Him into your boat?

5

Overcomers

Revelation 12:11 And they overcame and conquered him because of the blood of the Lamb and because of the WORD of their testimony, for they did not love their life and renounce their faith even when faced with death.

The enemy would like nothing better than for you and me to shut up; but when we have a testimony, we have power. Satan is ever before the Lord accusing us, but we have to know that we have power. We have power in our mouths and so we need to use it to combat the attacks of the enemy.

As professionals, some may think that we have it all together; that we are just fearless and go through without a worry in the world. I mean most of us walk upright with an air of confidence to some, maybe arrogance to others depending on your point of reference. The reality is, there are many times when we are so stricken with self-doubt that we are doing all that we could to hold it together. Have you ever had a situation where you took care of a difficult patient and went home and worried yourself to death about whether you did the right thing for the patient?

I have experienced this and have had to talk myself through it. Remind myself that what I did was the best for the patient and speak life over the patient. And this is the thing, we should remember that as believers, we hold a gift to speak life to our patients. We are equipped with the Word of God and our words matter and have power in the lives of our patients. The best moments I have had, are those moments when I speak the Word to a patient whose soul was crying out. What they needed was ministry to their soul and not so much their body. This moment to shift the dynamic gives the patients and us an opportunity to experience victory in the spirit realm, a defeat of the enemy, self-doubt.

PRAYER: Lord thank you that words have power. Thank you for allowing me to speak life into the atmosphere and encourage those who are discouraged and fearful. Even when I am afraid, I remember that your word is true. I remember the words that You speak over me. Thank you for that, in Jesus Name. Amen.

Prayer Journal: When have you most doubted your abilities? How did you overcome?

6

His Excellency

Psalm 8:1,4 O Lord, our Lord, how excellent is Your name in all the earth! You have set Your Glory on the heavens. What is man that You are mindful of him and the son of man that You care for him? Yet You have made him but a little lower than God and You have crowned him with glory and honor. You made him to have dominion over the works of Your hands; You have put all things under his feet.

God is excellent, He is a God of Excellence and He made us in His image and so by default we are people of Excellence. Because we may not always walk in our identity does not change our identity. A puppy can dress up like a cat all day long, can squeak like a mouse, but the essence of that puppy is all dog!

We can walk outside of our calling, we can act outside of our mission but what God has called us to, is SURE. We are wired for dominion, that does not change, and will not change. What God has done is sure and final. It is up to us now to step into destiny. We have to take off the leftovers of our insecurities and put on the fine livery of dominion.

Harrison's Principles of Internal Medicine is the go-to bible for those of us in Internal Medicine. The more you read and practice, the less you actually reference the text because it becomes a part of your fundamental knowledge base. It is a premium reference text; everything you need to know about Internal Medicine is in Harrison's. Much of what you will encounter in medicine, you measure against the knowledge you have gained in the text.

Likewise, the Bible is the reference text for everything human. The more we read it and digest it, the more we embody its tenets. The Word lives and grows in us. If we are to treat the body, we cannot treat it devoid of addressing spirit and soul issues. Furthermore, we cannot treat the body outside of the Creator. We were created with such intricate excellence that it will be wise to not consult with the One who crafted our genius.

As we treat each patient, we realize that it is not a "one plan fits all", because as individual as the patient is, so it is with the treatment plan. We must reference the original manuscript and the Creator of that manuscript as we create a treatment and healing plan for each patient. If we are to truly treat the body, we cannot do so outside of the one who created it.

> **PRAYER:** Father thank you for taking time to make me so wonderful. Thank you for your attention to details and for knitting together such greatness in me. May I continue to go from glory to glory through the guidance of the Holy Spirit. As I treat each patient, help me to see them in the uniqueness in which you have created them. In Jesus Name, Amen.

Prayer Journal: What are some unique features about you? How can you augment it to glory God?

7

His Goodness

Psalm 23:5-6 You prepare a table before me in the presence of my enemies. You have anointed and refreshed my head with oil; My cup overflows. Surely goodness and mercy and unfailing love shall follow me all the days of my life, And I shall dwell forever [throughout all my days] in the house and in the presence of the Lord.

I am thankful that these twins, Goodness and Mercy, run after us and are assigned to follow us all the days of my life. No matter what is going on in our lives. No matter how bad it seems, goodness follows; no matter how dark the night mercy follows. Our walk with the Lord is not always sugar coated but in these dark times I am convinced more than ever of His love. In the verse 5, it says, He anoints our head with OIL and our cup runs over. The oil is the anointing and the anointing is the ability to do what we have been assigned to do. It is our superhero covering. God gives us the unique ability, i.e., anointing to figure out medical mysteries. The anointing puts us in a place of surplus if we tap into it. We will never run out. So, God has us dripping with His anointing to get through any adversity and any resistance we would encounter. We have a built-in surplus.

We should also remember that the oil that comes from the olive gets out through crushing. There is a deep press that happens to get the oil out. We will have to undergo some pressing but we must remember that His Mercy and Goodness are with us, for the rest of our lives. Becoming a physician is its own special crushing! Lord knows, it was not easy. But we have persevered and thrived in it all.

We have thrived through the sleepless nights, the never ending pages, rounding on patients when we ourselves needed to be a patient, crying in the call room after experiencing yet another micro aggression, a patient dying after working so hard to keep them alive, studying for boards while trying to maintain some semblance of normalcy. We have come out on the other side; there is another side. Thank God.

As we walk through life, let us remember that we are covered AND His Goodness and Mercy are chasing after us! He has already called us and who He calls, He equips.

PRAYER: Father thank you for the ability to fulfill the call. Thank you that on this day I will tap into your power and allow you to flow through me. In Jesus Name. Amen.

Prayer Journal: What are some of the hardest moments you have endured. How did you make it through?

8

Relentless

Psalm 130:1-6 From the depths of despair, O Lord, I call for your help. Hear my cry, O Lord. Pay attention to my prayer. Lord, if you kept a record of our sins, who, O Lord, could ever survive? But you offer forgiveness, that we might learn to fear you. I am counting on the Lord; yes, I am counting on him. I have put my hope in his word. I long for the Lord more than sentries long for the dawn, yes, more than sentries long for the dawn. O Israel, hope in the Lord; for with the Lord there is unfailing love.

God's love is unfailing. He is an amazing coach. When I trained for competition, we pressed our bodies beyond the limit, all in hope of being the fastest and winning. As an athlete I would rise to do 4am runs in subzero temperatures. I did not always FEEL like getting out of my warm cozy bed to brave the elements, but I did it. I did it because there was a bigger vision ahead of me. Sometimes it felt like there was no way I can complete the workout but every time I pressed, I finished. I remember how I would start with one weight and then graduate to the next weight. I documented this progress with my trainers because sometimes when we graduate to leg pressing 400 lbs., we forget that 100 pounds used to be hard.

With every workout, I got stronger. On Race Day, I sailed through the competition because of that preparation. Preparation met the mandate as a friend of mine says.

It is likewise in medicine, we started out having to look up everything, then gradually we were able to write prescriptions without looking up the dose as we became so familiar with it. We are able to recognize patterns and devise treatment plans without looking it up. We have learned some lessons the hard way, lessons we will never forget. We have spent sleepless nights, pushed our body beyond self-set limits, crammed for exams, repeat and repeat. Rushing to see 18 patients before rounds, memorizing everything you can about that patient and then looking up their conditions, with the mind to be able to answer any question the attending may ask. The first day of call ever in your life, it was so difficult but now after hundreds of calls, we wake up like nothing, give the order and go back to sleep. We see growth. We have grown.

And it is the same with our faith, faith grows in adversity. There is no way that we grow faith outside of trials. Keep pressing, keep reading the Word, keep reminding yourself of the memorial stones you have laid. God is faithful. He knows that you have it in you to finish this course. If He did not believe you could finish the course, He would not have put you in the race. Do not give up on yourself. You are a winner.

PRAYER: Heavenly Father, thank you for the hard times, thank you for the pressing, thank you for adversities. Thank you that through it all, you never left me, and you will never leave me. Thank you that I am stronger because of it. Thank you for your unfailing love through these times. In Jesus Name, Amen.

Prayer Journal: Can you journal your progress? Start from the beginning and outline key points of growth.

9

Stand In Place

*Ephesians 6:11-18 Put on the full armor of God
[for His precepts are like the splendid armor of a
heavily armed soldier], so that you may be able to
[successfully] stand up against all the schemes and
the strategies and the deceits of the devil. For our
struggle is not against flesh and blood [contending
only with physical opponents], but against the
rulers, against the powers, against the world forces
of this [present] darkness, against the spiritual
forces of wickedness in the heavenly (supernatural)
places. Therefore, put on the complete armor
of God, so that you will be able to [successfully]
resist and stand your ground in the evil day [of
danger], and having done everything [that the
crisis demands], to stand firm [in your place,
fully prepared, immovable, victorious]. So stand
firm and hold your ground, having [a]tightened*

the wide band of truth (personal integrity, moral courage) around your waist and having put on the breastplate of righteousness (an upright heart), and having strapped on your feet the gospel of peace in preparation [to face the enemy with firm-footed stability and the readiness produced by the good news]. Above all, lift up the [protective] [c]shield of faith with which you can extinguish all the flaming arrows of the evil one. And take the helmet of salvation, and the sword of the Spirit, which is the Word of God. With all prayer and petition pray [with specific requests] at all times [on every occasion and in every season] in the Spirit, and with this in view, stay alert with all perseverance and petition [interceding in prayer] for all God's people.

The Word tells us that we are not fighting a regular battle and outlines the armor that God has given us to fight the battle. If we are not fighting a regular battle, then we are not going to have regular armor! God has given us supernatural gear; we have A grade gear! But like anything, we will never know how effective it is unless we USE it.

Our body has its army as well, our immune system is a bad team of defenders. When an invader enters, the system mobilizes as ONE. There is no wavering on their position as it relates to defending the body.

It is important for us to KNOW who we are and as the Word says in the amplified version, STAND IN PLACE. WE must KNOW who we are and to whom we belong when we go into battle.

We know that we belong to the Lord and He has never lost a battle! EVER! His track record is spotless;

what a great commander in chief to have. Not only has He never lost a battle, but He guarantees our win in Him! He guaranteed our win on the cross with Jesus. So, we do not go into this fight as victims. We stand in victory before the battle has even been fought. The battle after all is the Lord's.

Enemies love to play intimidation tactics. But we stand confident in who and whose we are. As you go about today, STAND IN PLACE. Your Place; own your place and space. You are the head and not the tail. The first and not the last, the righteousness of God in Christ Jesus, more than an overcomer, joint heirs with Christ. And so much more.

Prayer: Father we thank you for positioning us to win. We are here to take win in your name. We will not be intimidated by the enemy. We will not shrink back. As you command, we follow, fearlessly, with full confidence in You. Thank you that the victory is already won. In Jesus Name. Amen.

Prayer Journal: Do you remember a time where you forgot who you were and allowed circumstances to intimidate you to the point where you did not recognize yourself? How did you get out of it? What will you do to make sure you stand in place?

10

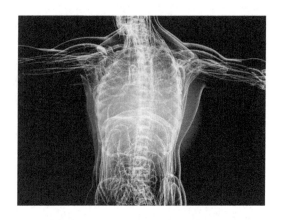

Presence without Pretense

Hebrews 4:14-16 So then, since we have a great High Priest who has entered heaven, Jesus the Son of God, let us hold firmly to what we believe. This High Priest of ours understands our weaknesses, for he faced all of the same testings we do, yet he did not sin. So, let us come boldly to the throne of our gracious God. There we will receive his mercy, and we will find grace to help us when we need it most.

Because our Lord has been there and done that and has not sinned, we can go before Him without pretense. We can enter His Presence without Pretense because He already knows what we are dealing with. He is already tuned into our issues. I love it that our Lord is relatable. We are the ones that make Him seem inaccessible, but He is so relatable. He made every effort to come down and walk among us and gave His very life so that He can intercede for us. Jesus was chilling at the well, kicking it with the woman with many husbands even though He knew her lifestyle was frowned upon. He even went to the party and turned it out with some wine. Jesus was not afraid to break every tradition so He can relate to us. He incited us to level up without putting us down. I love that about Him.

I have said to many medical students and residents that as physicians and physician leaders, we should never be ashamed to ask questions. We need grace to persevere the training. We should not fall into the trap that we know everything and pretend because it is ultimately dangerous to our patients and ourselves. Humility is demonstrated in naming our deficit and working to bridge that knowledge gap. God has given us Grace to persevere, even when we do not necessarily like what we see. He is leveling us up without putting us down.

> **PRAYER: Father thank you that I can come to you, naked and unashamed.** Thank you that you do not show me my shortcomings to shame me but rather to bring me closer to You. It is an opportunity to allow you into the most secret places of my life. I love that you love me. Help me

Prayer Journal: What have you been holding back from God?

11

Here I am, Send Me

Isaiah 6:8 Also I hear the voice of the Lord saying, whom shall I send? And who will go for us? Then I said I, here am I send me

If we do not go, then who? I remember in 1994 laying on my face in prayer at church crying out to the Lord and saying the very same thing that Isaiah said. When you are in the Presence of the Lord and under the anointing fully surrendered, you say whatever the Holy Spirit in you will say. What we do not realize is our going and doing is not under our own strength. About a year after, I was going to Trinidad. This was all before medical school. I felt very strongly that the Lord wanted me to go to the streets and share the gospel. I thought, "of course".

I got home and the day after I arrived, I felt the Lord say…TODAY. I cannot tell you the FEAR that all of a sudden raised up in me. I stood in my grandmother's bedroom and started to cry because here I was in Trinidad, in familiar ground where people knew me, and God wanted me to go preaching on the streets! I KNEW that I could not disobey but I was so afraid. I called my prayer partner and we prayed together. She was an older seasoned Christian and she pumped me up in the spirit with very specific instructions. Shower, dress, go to the city and ask God where to stand. I did just that. Went to the town, the Holy Spirit instructed me to go to the main street, Frederick Street. I thought, "Really God?!" I was hoping I would be sent to some obscure street where the likelihood of me running into any of my friends would be low. I did as I felt lead to do and as I stood on Frederick Street, building up the courage to speak, I saw a vendor and her crew. I struck up a conversation with them. I told her why I was there, and it turned out she was a believer. She and her team prayed for me. It was as though I got a shot of java, and before I knew it, I started to speak. That day, I lead two young boys to the Lord. I felt so light, so free afterwards! We have to learn to depend on the Holy Spirit, the power of the Holy Spirit to carry out the mandate. If we do not go, then who? We are the hands and feet and mouth…we are the BODY of Christ and so that means, it is up to us to do the work that the Father desires to bring His name Glory. That vendor is today one of my friends running a very successful NGO which God has allowed me to bless and which has blessed so many in return.

My coming into medicine was a perfect combination of my love of science and my deep faith in God. I also have a supportive tribe around me who encouraged me even when I told myself stories of failure. Isn't it amazing how we try to talk ourselves out of our destiny? I see no difference between the two (science and faith) because fundamentally, everything that happens in the spirit is manifested in the natural. It is a natural thing for me to incorporate these beliefs in my practice. It is my faith in God that keeps me in medicine and allows me to stretch beyond my own natural abilities. It is this faith that allows me to step out boldly and minister to patients in their deep places. I am intentional in using my faith in healing. This is why I because a doctor, so I can glorify God.

The team in medicine is so important. We support each other, we complement each other's role. We lean on each other's wisdom.

So many times, we are living beneath what he has called us to do and be. We have become comfortable with complacency. I said here I am, and He sent me. Where are you? Will you step out and follow Him all the way?

> **PRAYER: Father in the Name of Jesus, I know that your election and calling are sure. Thank you for giving me courage to do what you have called me to do. Thank you that you have given me everything I need to fulfill the mandate and the call. I say yes, here I am. In Jesus Name.**

Prayer Journal: How will you glorify God in your practice today?

12

You Are Welcome

Revelation 3:20 Behold, I stand at the door [of the church] and continually knock. If anyone hears My voice and opens the door, I will come in and eat with him (restore him), and he with Me.

I know I am not the only one who has seen someone coming to the door who I did not want to let in, and I completely ignored the doorbell or the knock on the door. That is for the unwanted visitor. Jesus on the other hand is not just any ordinary visitor but truth is many still do not want to let Him in. Many still hide because they are not "prepared" to receive Him, or they need to "fix up" before they can let Him in. But remember He is a friend that is closer than a brother; He is our Redeemer. He already knows what is in us.

So how do you let Him in? By praying, reading the Word, doing as He did in the earth and ministering to the least among us. Sometimes the least are those who do not know Him as Lord and Savior; they may have all the world accoutrements but lack the most valuable commodity and that is relationship with Christ.

Some may say, well how do I know it's Him? How do I know when Jesus is knocking? The more you spend time with someone the more you KNOW them and the subtleties in their movements. The way the Lord may communicate with you, may not be the way He communicates with me. When you have HISTORY with someone, you can give a certain look that they know exactly what you are trying to say. For me, whenever I see a hummingbird, I pay attention because it is a certain confirmation that the Lord wants my attention, or it may be a question I just asked. I find Him in the Word and in prayer when I sit still and listen, I hear Him. He is in a fleeing thought. I find Him in nature. I see Him int he seasons. There is just a burning in your heart when He is near. There are times that something in you just KNOWS; you cannot put your finger on it, it is not something you can truly articulate with words. The scripture mentions on several occasions that the disciples' hearts "burned within them" when Jesus was around, something about this person they met resonated. The point is we need to spend time with Him and learn His ways. Time spent with the Lord is always rich, you are always left in a better place and space after His fellowship.

I have learned to allow Him into my practice of medicine. I have invited him to define the art of medicine in my practice. It has led to restoration not just in my patients but in myself.

> **Prayer: Father thank you for this time to sit and sup with you. May my eyes be open to see and hear you and learn the subtleties of your ways. Prepare my heart to receive you, you are welcome in here Jesus. Amen.**

Prayer Journal: How are you preparing a place for Jesus?

13

Closer Than A Friend

John 15:13-14 No one has greater love (nor stronger commitment) than to lay down his own life for his friends. You are my friends if you keep on doing what I command you.

His love never runs empty, it gets sweeter and sweeter with time!

In this day and age, we see many use the word friend and it is used loosely. Everyone is a Facebook "Friend", what is that even? I am reminded by the scripture in John that friendship is a heart matter and asks for deep life-giving commitment. It is more than word of mouth; it is couched with action. I had a call with two of my friends recently. We talked dreams, fears, joys, whatever was on our hearts. We spoke without fear of judgment or betrayal. One started out telling me she was thinking of this major event and she knew that she could share that with me, and it would go no further. The other shared how she was stretching herself outside of her comfort zone. We have a history of denying ourselves for each other, giving the best of ourselves so that the other is uplifted, of carrying each other's business with honor.

Our body is set up for interdependence it is the only life-giving force and so is the Body of Christ, we are set up for interdependence. My head will never reach its potential without the neck and so on. The interdependence is the life-giving force. And even so, if one part of the Body is hurt, the entire body rushes to aid.

Jesus showed that He is indeed a friend and gave the ultimate...He gave His very life. He would not ask us to do something that He himself didn't do. When we lay down our life for Him, we show ourselves to be His friends. When we follow the commandments, we show ourselves to be His friends.

Today let us reestablish our friendship lines with Christ. Let us accept His friend request. And let us be a friend that we would want.

> **PRAYER: Father thank you for our relationship. Thank you that I can come to you for anything and you will not condemn me or make light of what concerns me. I appreciate your friendship and pray that I will use the power of the Holy Spirit whom you left me to do your will. In Jesus Name. Amen**

Prayer Journal: What does friendship mean to you? How deep are your friendships? Would you lay down your life for Christ?

14

One Love

John 17:6-11 I have revealed you[a] to those whom you gave me out of the world. They were yours; you gave them to me, and they have obeyed your word. Now they know that everything you have given me comes from you. For I gave them the words you gave me, and they accepted them. They knew with certainty that I came from you, and they believed that you sent me. I pray for them. I am not praying for the world, but for those you have given me, for they are yours. All I have is yours, and all you have is mine. And glory has come to me through them. I will remain in the world no longer, but they are still in the world, and I am coming to you. Holy Father, protect them by the power of your name, the name you gave me, so that they may be one as we are one

A s a physician, I am intimately aware of the interplay of the body and all its parts. Every part needs the other. The right foot is no good without the left foot and the heart needs the arteries to carry out its function just as the brain is useless unless it has the body. Every part needs the other. Can you imagine if you disconnected your arm from your shoulder? How well does that work? Does either fulfill its mission?

And so, it is with the Body of Christ, we NEED each other. We must believe that without the other, we cannot be fulfilled. There is ONE CHURCH, ONE BODY. We have compartmentalized to the point of death. Dead churches circulating leads to a dead Body. In medicine we contain an infection by doing "source control"; that means we immediately address the problematic area otherwise it will affect and infect the entire body.

In medicine, there is a condition called compartment syndrome, if untreated, it is sure death to the tissue. It is a painful condition wherein the pressure within the muscles builds to dangerous levels. Such pressure can decrease blood flow. Without blood flow, the muscles and nerves are starved of nourishment and oxygen. In medical school, I learned the 5 P's of compartment syndrome. Pain, Pallor, Pulseless, Paresthesia and Paralysis. Let's address each P separately.

1. Pain: When a part of the body hurts, it is important that we address is right away. Compartment syndrome is due to injury, if that injury is not addressed then it leads to the other Ps. When members of the body are hurting, it is important to get healing to that area right away otherwise we risk losing the whole body.

2. Pallor: Because there is little blood flow to the area, it loses its shine, its color. When as a body we do not address our pain and allow the healing virtue of the Lord to come to that area, we begin to show our pain rather than His glory.

3. Pulselessness: A lack of a pulse, usually denotes a lack of life, or a lack of blood flow. If the pain is not addressed, we have a matter of impending death. There is no blood flow or limited blood flow to the area. The tissue then starves.

4. Paresthesia: There is a loss of feeling. Where there is no blood there is no life and lack of feeling. The numbness that we exhibit as we walk through trauma will eventually lead to #5

5. Paralysis: Damage is done. The limb cannot move or function in its calling if it is without the life flowing in it. At this stage, this part of the body is ineffective, and eventually will spread to the rest of the body.

The treatment is surgery; cutting open the compartment to allow the muscle tissue room to decrease the pressure and allow for blood flow again. All of this can be avoided if we address the pain head-on. All of us, as one. Until we recognize the importance of the Other and realize that the Other is US, we will fail at the commission. Let us always remember that we are connected.

But I want to bring this even closer to home, as physicians we have also done a job of compartmentalizing our lives. We separate our spiritual life from our professional life because in most of where we practice there is an application of the false separation of church and state. We have endured the pain that is inherent in medical education, including micro aggressions and racism, sexism and all manner of misogyny. We have seen patients hurt and while we hurt too, we have not stopped to process that pain. And so, we have this pain buildup. We have piled our pain. We switch out and continue on our lives "normally", not stopping to fully confront the pain and invite the Holy Spirit in to heal. We practice to the point of developing emotional compartment syndrome which creates a callous so thick that now we are separated from our "first love", people and medicine. Unless we recognize this, we too can become a statistic. We too will lose our way in this art that we love so much. Let us stop for a moment and care for ourselves and reset. Let us acknowledge our wounds and trauma so we can truly move forward in health.

Prayer: Father forgive me for forgetting that it is not just about me. Forgive me for not realizing that I am part of the Body. Let me hurt when one hurts. Let me be kind to my own self and address my pain when it is before me. Let me demonstrate daily a love for the Body of Christ by loving you, myself and my brother and sisters in Christ. In Jesus Name. Amen.

Prayer Journal: Where are you hurting? How can you start the healing process?

Made in the USA
Middletown, DE
02 November 2022

14005759R00031